Indexical Elegies
-- Jon Paul Fiorentino.

Coach House Books
-- Toronto.

Published with the generous assistance of the Canada Council for the Arts and the Ontario Arts Council. Coach House Books also acknowledges and appreciates the support of the Government of Canada through the Canada Book Fund and the Government of Ontario through the Ontario Book Publishing Tax Credit.

LIBRARY AND ARCHIVES CANADA CATALOGUING IN PUBLICATION

Fiorentino, Jon Paul
 Indexical elegies / Jon Paul Fiorentino.

Poems.
ISBN 978-1-55245-234-9

 I. Title.

PS8561.I585164 2010   c811'.6   C2010-903887-8

For Marisa Grizenko

Elizabeth Conway
     (A Montreal Suite)

the echo deferred, dispersal, the night declines its relays.
To explore: the ultimate intimate elsewhere.

                           – Nicole Brossard

The high ones die, die. They die. You look up and who's
there?

                     – John Berryman ('Dream Song 36')

Life, friend, is boring. We must not say so.

                     – John Berryman ('Dream Song 14')

ELIZABETH CONWAY

We visit Elizabeth Conway on Sundays, select Mondays
and stumble, habitually untied
above Snowdon, Mile End

We take the long way on these days
release captivating missives
wake up later

Maybe croon names like Edith McCord,
Ellie Dowling, or maybe not, still we
drive ourselves civic

One day, road-tripping ourselves
to l'Epiphanie, QC, we will
turn around just in time

Look for home firmly planted
on a Sunday, select Mondays, too easy to parse
and so still, so departed

There's a Montreal I'm
beginning to see and
you're everywhere in it, Conway.

Notre-Dame-des-Neiges Cemetery, Spring 2008

JOBLESS WONDERBOY

Jobless little wonder
needs his antibiotics

Jobber never leaves
never earns his lesions

Got paper and markers
and motherfucking whiteout

Listen, sent you a text
message in 1983

One day you'll get it

MENTHOLISM

Cold is your gift
spend countless hours grifting

Sole proprietorship
of these barricades

Close eyes
pretend we have talent

Not swayed
too into too craven

Can't hold liquor
can't hold sobriety

Smoke Craven Menthols
not sure why

Get frigid
ride late night

Last call
scratch open white scabs

Walk-in therapist sees you
there you are

Don't have a problem
in writing

Need a
room in which to brood

An adjacent
room from which to watch

So hard to keep
the stories straight

This poem makes
sure of that

MONTREAL SONG

And then she said
being despotic is almost
as rewarding as being enlightened

Then he said
I love everything about
you except your company

And then we all agreed
that power politics were
depressing

POLICE DRIVE HATCHBACKS

Ask for cocaine
sane currency
petulant
continent

Walk the
strip-mined outlet mall
make eye contact
with retailers

Enter hostel
fall asleep
to your
bitmap

One weak moment
that won't
stop
happening

WHAT'S THE WORST THAT COULD HAPPEN, COURTNEY?

She slides out of a launderette
No, wait. She struts out of a café

Check that. She stumbles out of a bus
Or not. She steps out of a bank

Too dull. She stirs out of a dream
That sucks. She slips out of a clinic

The washer is old; the smoke is thick
the transit is slow; the credit is wrecked
the fear is real; the doctor is sick

Her clothes are stained; her coffee is cold
her transfer is lost; her money is low
her mind is made up; her pills do not work

Shouldn't think so
I've been so thoughtless

Mispronounce *hegemony*
that's nothing

Announce too candidly
my candidacy

Something I hardly know
protects itself from being happy

Years saunter by, increasingly devoid of lyric
thankful, they say, wheezing:

It's all about your breath all about you breathing
every beta male needs a better Maud Gonne

Very well aware: close readings
find me lacking or treading or tactless or fruitless

But here's something: it's 4:07 a.m.
you are asleep; and I am in the midst of

an historical narrative

CRUELTY-AS-TREND

Suppose you supplant someone
suppose it's not unwelcome

Suppose you uproot or unseed or unseat him, that
certain someone, and discover cruelty-as-trend in the process

Suppose you have an art project to work on now, but no
matter, because you haven't the ethic or ethics

Suppose you understand process a little better now
but don't feel convertible in your own skin

Suppose you will need this, this making strange
this continual troubling

Suppose you've been found out and you find out you
don't care. Suppose you process this supposition

GRIFT ECONOMY

Manage to in syntax
Xerox massage it

Bedsores soothe, bedsitters swoon
Back when X cared about things

Intentions pulped or stapled
closer

So close to sleep
yet so closed

The epiphany changes
whenever the font does

It's easy to look down on you
from this basement suite

MONTREAL IS AN IDIOT

in October as the slumlords
slur the ruddy Plateau

Third-hand bicycles
gun-toting angels
last last cigarettes
activist boyfriends
projectivist adjuncts
protectionist tracts

And at night the mayor
gets colder than we could
ever imagine

And we love him
and we love her

I'M PULLING FOR YOUR NARRATIVE

It's a trope
I think you know it

The ATM looks lovely tonight
if you believe in the word *lovely*

You kill an adjective
and then

The word *lovely* wakes
you up at 4 p.m. and says:

It's been a while
it's lost its charm

You sleep too much
you drink too long

CELLPHONE GLITTER

Write long line
angry young kick

Gain Saint Joe; lose Saint Joe
daddy bank robber sputter

Stroke cellphone glitter
rock suffocate coke

Protest too much
protest tumult

Drain muse battery
suck fake epic on
prick strike for

Lo, the tired are punch-drunk
let's get 'em, Uncle Job

ABJECTIVE

Abject stirring
prose project stalled

Stab injection
the wrecked and the appalled

When does the second head
drop

When does the adjective
leave you alone

Jab injure
zero

When does the crop
come?

MENTHOL HYMN

What do you mean *right on?*
extract life menthol
what do you mean *unhappy?*
excursion retreat menthol
what do you mean *my fault?*
cure yourself again menthol
what do you mean *your fault?*
children crave sick menthol
what do you mean *not now?*
make it new menthol
what do you mean *hurtful?*
hey it's only menthol
what do you mean *virgin?*
shame on you menthol
what do you mean *never?*
preen espouse menthol
what do you mean *twenty bucks?*
sexually transmuted menthol
what do you mean *leaving?*
montreal city menthol
what do you mean *verb?*
aim low miss menthol
what do you mean *noun?*
first thought best menthol
what do you mean *problem?*
literal mean menthol
what do you mean *dead locution?*
liked your recent menthol
what do you mean *archive?*
it's not you it's menthol

CAUTIOUSLY SOLIPSISITIC

If self is dishappy
cautionary tale stuck on repeat

If posed self is paused
solitary drive drivel

If drive is inward
sociological, heteronormative slapstick

If you feel you can drive it home
power outage, gender outrage

If triage is trendy
crack and hiss Christmas illness

Don't let yourself let
everyone know you get paid

TELEGRAPHIA

Real ones happen when you are post-telegraphic
almost at sleep

Real ones happen when the mind trips post-
Sapphic

Real ones are itches and pre-dream clutter
they happen shallow

Dream curvature and whisper inertial
the mind wakes up at dreadful times

Deep
post-happen

DO YOU FALL IN LOVE AT THE DROP OF HAPPY?

Do you fall in love at the drop of happy?
are you brink? did you clean?
do you miss yourself? are you dripping?
you are taken for

Did you fail?
are you held? did you internet café?
do you slum? are you napping?
you were missed

Do you last?
are you heading there? did it out you?
do you lure? are you dropping?
you miss bugs

Do you lull?
are your friends? did you pulp?
do you mean this? are we meant for this?
yes

SELF-STORAGE

Laminated name tags everywhere everywhere
       shelf space for the wicked timid

Bottles tremble in November treble
       everyone dying or leaving or straying

Meanwhile quiz-takers make some sonic sense
       pitch perfect prose, retail summons

Sermon perfect-lit compartments down
       oh value-added mainstays whisper

This name tag, that toe tag
       November swallows the widowed

Comedic grievers mutter lame phonemes:
       did you hear the one about the laminated coffin?

Heard it –
       big year for that joke

POLYCLINIQUE

Find your place –
a local, measure the paces

Arrive with head down
headlong into intent

Lace the notion
with disrigorous play and ploy, somehow

Put the idea under chloroform
deliberate and douse the thing

in a flow of solvents
not as remedy, nor as spark nor wick

but as strategic sublimation
conspicuously consumed

Trick your dreams into commonplace routine –
matte offerings of concrete nouns that ease and shame

Stitch up a coterie of kindreds
note where connections are severed

Finally sew lazily, forcefully. See the language
gnaw at its sutures as you go

Tip well

There is no truth
but in dead event, shaken, stunned

I miss everybody

— Gilbert Sorrentino

The index is physically connected with its object; they make
an organic pair.

— Charles Sanders Peirce

Indexical Elegies

Little Lucifer falls
despite listless prayers

The palliative strain
and cigarette drama

Don't fuck this up
with your feelings

Went to sleep without
him

Tried to dream him
back

But it's zero sum the
summer

Nothing cold about it
it's just that

The closer I come to loving
the closer I edge into elegy

Shh. There are
poets trying to die

HYMN

Wicked tension bloom
blast wistful tenor
tensor black winter

Wilted tenure blessed
blown window terser
tepid bloke wither

Wilful tested blame
bliss winded temper
tester bleach widows

CSP

What is a sign?

Some grand logic?

Some cradling?

HYMN

Method whistle sense stab
tenure rapist tract traces
mother split pencil stretch
trainer nonce tensor spurt

Clever brine tory magic
branded libel scandal lice
cloister sacred wax mental
bail snap willing scoundrel

CSP

A critick of arguments

A most necessary question

So many meanings –

An injury to language to add a new one

The word 'I' is apparently
an essential indexical unit

I hate
this

I lost you in November
and if time isn't subjective

it's November again and I am
appalled I grieve

Time is subjunctive
I am your index now

HYMN

Hitches in stance prog
jab injure ginger strut
hinges on hand hips
jar conjure sidle walk

Graft pilfer menthol mask
draper mortar swagger lean
great button tender grime
drifter bindle twist cap

CSP

Primary protegé

Secondary supplicant

Mediatory muse

Every failure follows from a failure

Memory is kind
kindness kills
my em dash is tired

Verbal version comes
iPod wrecks the soundtrack
vice conjugates the visit

Indicate indecent indices

HYMN

Nab when glottal wince
lick limber water tread
nick nature nurture this
lie code ethics shift

Act yourself skip langue
icon freight measure safe
ask symbol fissure pose
index metric like nest

CSP

Indices and indexicals indicate the direction

Icons bore us to death

Insofar as we can see

Every sign, rote signs all the way to hospice

You were my only Terran

Shift subaltern
lonely all shoot mental
shun St. Dominique
why rent mini-Terran
shawl fist alternative

Slow eon tool name
lull yell lamental
saltwater hymen
wall comely DIY
stall innate comedy

HYMN

so lisper deeper plebe
bass range glitch crackle
sect tenor pocket tone
bitch sever gloss pitch

fever range check in
Xerox line strange break
fractal knowledge sever it
Xbox lever pulley snare

Spectral analysis

Embolum – bolt lock –
thrown together

Parabolum – collateral lock –
thrown beside

Hypobolum – platen lock –
thrown underneath

The fall takes forever

Still thrown for a loss

My sincere apologists

They knew him
like

So stunned by
your

And how dare
it

Because we never have
very

But if s/he
only

Troll, you
trawl

Shhh

I object to your secondness
your leaving
autumn slippage
yellowed paper
small
pressed

Sick of signage
turn left at Ayer's Cliff
stick to the side road
trail any direction

All roads, side roads
all text, signage

All seasons, autumn
all memories, winter

Steven dreamed of you the very second
you died

(So the poem goes)
and you may have visited him

But I'm pretty sure you don't believe
in poems

Home is where the arc is
home is where the arch is

Begin with digression
rerun of the archons

Alone in ink and whiskey
wasted well on paper

Obliterate this order
eliminate signatures, signifiers

Make it sense –
home is where the chart is

Domiciliation dance
constrained in little rooms

Tied up in theory
so cold on consignment

Dust gathers
librarians dust

He's dead

Too much displacement
not enough condensation

You have texts
to be completed

Left them on a
jump drive for us

Archive key

Terrible symmetry
sorrowful telemetry

Start again with
signatory stature

Make nice with
old signposts

Make strange with
odd likenesses

Make new icons
drop old habits

Proceed without familial
consent

Rob,

Jay, Dave and I
stashed all the expensive
whiskey at your wake.

Not sorry,
Jonny

It's over

The invalid townships
insist

The sickening tenured
posit

Let it rest
no more mythologies

Stash pain
in a volume of poetry

Where no one could possibly
find it

I miss everybody

Me too

Where are the other senses:
the sick twist of what you strain through metre

The feelings, notions, street corners, alcoves
jargonistics, sidewinders, string theories, me too

Flesh and no lungs appalling m'appelling
never no gerund me fixate when and recalling tome

Question for every sense and infinite use
despotism of the finite and drink it, slam it toward me

Yeah, Robert, I feel you, want you holding on
me too

Composed in 1946
compost in 4/4 time

Then
comprosed –
a new verb
wicked and defiant

Missing you

Send in the nouns

Transprairie
  (A Post-Prairie Suite)

The open prairie conceals a chasm.

— Robert Kroetsch

in that person is a site

dreaming of floods and rivers woke
            gagging

— Jessica Grim

TRANSPRAIRIE

       Please step away from the scene
nothing to be here

       It follows that the primary unit of poetry
in flatland is the line

       We have arrived: world class in our way –
our way is lost: we like it Rich, standby

       The dreams you don't know you know
and the dreams you know all too well

       You are tranced
I am incidental

       But in which kind of poetry
do we place our dead dreams?

INSTRUCTIONS FOR SPROUTING A POET IN WINNIPEG

It's non-arable land so go hydroponic
once you sprout, lay low
don't make eye contact with teachers or ministers

Shower three times a day
don't pray. There's no god in Winnipeg
there *is* an understaffed drop-in centre

Use fine-tip pens
red ink is more than fine
only write on receipts and parking tickets

Pitch a tent. Stay a while
but don't get comfortable
when they find out, lay low in Selkirk

When they forget, come back
or don't. But always remember:
they will forget you

INSTRUCTIONS FOR SPROUTING A POST-PRAIRIE POET IN WINNIPEG

Hydro sprout low
administer shower shovel
loyal writhe receipt

Accept sense tenting
sell member hideout
comfort brace remembrance

Get growl forget

PROCESSIONAL DEVELOPMENT
(talking points from the Winnipeg Leadership Symposium for Leaders, March 1994)

• What you need to know
• is the brain is so very good
• at picking stuff up.

• Are they really
• reading the labels?
• Really?

• Remember: the idea
• of the holy grail
• is viral.

- Fifty percent of readers
- will actually do something.
- That's a big number.
- If you think about percentages.

- Remember the soaps?
- Remember watching them?
- They were soap-driven!
- Remember the soaps.

- People love advertising.
- That's why
- they buy things.

- I will show you a chart
- that will knock you out
- literally.

- Think of it as a good workout.
- The name of the game
- is brand fitness.

- Is there an occasion
- that's not a purchase occasion?
- Maybe a funeral, but I don't think so.

- People always have rational
- passions and interests.
- Use them.

- If you probe popularity
- you will avoid playing
- hard to sell.

- The question
- is not 'why?'
- It's 'how come?'

- Just think about it:
- four percent penetration
- in just five seconds.
- Who doesn't want that?

LATCHKEYED

Sick of the trains
left the conscience

West of the Seine
dream the Albert

Prayer of the contingent
drone the late shift

Next to November
tell the mall to swell

Please the Perimeter
will straight lines

Pay homage at wholesale rate
rent-to-own disappointment

Croon any scrapyard
insulate the empties

Drive by the winter
sleep summerfall

Wake up furious, deadlocked
daydream latchkeyed

MIASMA MEDICATION

Take the North Main Car east
watch your strep

Selkirk Avenue and so on
sad insistence. Dark matters

How's your labour?
the smug get paid

The old dreams never die
never really lived

And some of us were
already someone

FAMOUS GREY CHEVETTE

Listen, when we were younger
we drove to the legislative buildings
in my famous grey Chevette and smoked
oil from bottle caps and bought
licks from street kids

And then we stared at the floodlights
until our retinas burned and the city
turned purple. We called it 'purple city' –
it was the only thing to do in Winnipeg

Do you remember this?
I think we were trying to
upgrade the city or go blind

ST. TRANSCONA

Transcona calls me at three in the morning
demanding a rewrite

But I've moved to St. James. And the *Free Press*
is already printed

The rivers are bingeing and purging again –
you see them only in the spring on the early news

This love moves toward something
at bonspiel speed

Consider yourself unhaloed in a trailer park
in St. Vital

You can lead a tourist to the Red River
but you can't make him drink himself to death

It's Saturday evening
I'll be at home, fucking up locutions

Sunday morning
I'll be at the floodway burying Saturday

STOP KNOWING HOW I AM

When the punchline is chlorine
you transgraze, catch cold

When the punchline is Advair
the side effect is death

When the punchline is adjunct
high on grad school Sudafed

When the punchline is prairie
periodicals spiral

When the punchline is hockey
tell it antiseptic

Stifled by dust
stunted by stricture

When the punchline is stop

CIVIC POEM

The poet, not as priest, but lover
The novelist, not as druid, but drunk

and shaking off careerist rust
but almost constantly shaking

and therefore displeased
but not completely displeasured

and, yes, health concerns
but no, not concerned

and they are tired of lessons
but the poets are pictograph sick

and how you get back from that fissure
but why you won't come

and the fissure divides the priests from the lovers
but the druids and the drunks mix implicit

and for some reason you like it in winter
but the adverbs returning

and the full rash
but the half-life left

and the votive, the semaphore
but the shrinking *ex voto*

and you know where to find you
but you hate civic poems

DYING IN WINNIPEG

Don't read me wrong –
I plan on dying in Winnipeg

In a strange way I
believe Winnipeg is where everything always dies:

Grandfathers, clock radios, Chevrolets
faith, journalists, fine-tip pens

Earle Nelson, hockey dads
your best friend from the old street …

I will let the rush-hour dust or the blowing
snow or the dance-hall fumes fill my lungs

I will simply wait, let my side-splitting body
fail under the flattering lights in the hallway

Of the underfunded Concordia Hospital
and don't dream of visiting

But listen, there's a show tonight
at the legion hall

And I have half a liver left and
a hatchback with a quarter tank

I'm not hard to be had

ACKNOWLEDGEMENTS

Elizabeth Bachinsky, Darren Bifford, Jason Camlot, Rachel Cyr, Tara Flanagan, Lilly Fiorentino, John Goldbach, David McGimpsey, Evan Munday, Sachiko Murakami, Ian Orti, Marisa Grizenko, Christina Palassio, Mike Spry, Darren Wershler.

My family.

Special thanks to Kevin Connolly, a wonderful editor.

Special thanks to Alana Wilcox for her friendship, guidance and patience.

The Nicole Brossard epigraph is from *Lovhers*.
The John Berryman epigraphs are from *Dream Songs*.
The Gilbert Sorrentino epigraph is from *Corrosive Sublimate*.
The Charles Sanders Peirce epigraph is from 'What Is a Sign?'
The Robert Kroetsch epigraph is from *The Hornbooks of Rita K.*
The Jessica Grim epigraph is from *Fray*.

Earlier versions of some of these poems have appeared in *The Walrus*, *Jacket*, *Prism*, *The Capilano Review*, *Scratching the Service: The Post-Prairie Landscape* (Plug-in Institute of Contemporary Art, 2008). 'Mentholism' and 'Little Grey Chevette' were originally written for broadcast on CBC Radio One. Thanks to CBC.

'Famous Grey Chevette' is for Christopher Charney.
'Transprairie' is for Louis Cabri, who suggested the term.
The 'Indexical Elegies' sequence is for Robert Allen, in memoriam.

Jon Paul Fiorentino is the author of the novel *Stripmalling*, which was shortlisted for the Paragraphe Hugh MacLennan Prize for Fiction, and three poetry collections, including *The Theory of the Loser Class*, which was shortlisted for the A. M. Klein Prize. He lives in Montreal, where he teaches writing at Concordia University, edits *Matrix* magazine and runs Snare Books.

Typeset in My Underwood and Adobe Caslon
Printed and bound at the Coach House on bpNichol Lane, 2010

This print run includes a limited edition of 52 geographically challenged
copies, lettered and signed by the author.

Edited by Kevin Connolly
Designed by Alana Wilcox
Author photo by Marisa Grizenko

Coach House Books
80 bpNichol Lane
Toronto M5S 3J4
Canada

416 979 2217
800 367 6360

mail@chbooks.com
www.chbooks.com